Ottawa

Irving Weisdorf & Co. Ltd.

Ottawa then and now. A history and a city to be proud of.

The Nation's Capital

Believe it or not - Ottawa is more than just government bureaucrats and a history lesson.

It's a city with a past, and a fascinating one at that. Not that long ago, Ottawa was a bawdy, even belligerent town.

For thousands of years, natives used the mighty Ottawa River as a highway, but history wasn't recorded there until 1613, when French explorer Samuel de Champlain, and hundreds of European traders, travelled that same route.

Things stayed relatively quiet until the early 1800s, when Wright's Town (now Hull) was born. It took Philemon Wright, a United Empire Loyalist from Massachusetts, to see money could be made from the forest. Thanks to Napoleon's blockade in the Baltic Sea, the British Navy couldn't get the

timber it needed from Scandinavia and Canadian lumber was soon crossing the Atlantic.

Troops travelling the St. Lawrence River from Montreal to Kingston and back were being hit hard by American soldiers, but there was no safe alternative. The Rideau Canal gave them hope when construction started around 1826, and it proved a solid option when it was finished in 1832. During those years, development heated up on the Ottawa side of the river and the Rideau Canal is still considered one of the 19th century's greatest engineering feats.

Ottawa: Canada's government and diplomatic capital, where ten provinces and two territories are federally represented.

While overseeing Rideau Canal construction, Colonel By laid out Bytown's streets.

In time, Bytown was christened Ottawa, although, no one can agree on the true meaning of the word Ottawa. Taken from a tribe of Algonquin Indians, some say Ottawa means "traders", others maintain Ottawa stands for "people of the forest". Apparently, even the Indians themselves aren't sure of the word's origin.

This city, and its name, remained the seat of controversy, becoming Canada's capital in 1857. History says Queen Victoria hoped that Ottawa would help defuse the fierce rivalry between the French and English-speaking populations by virtue of its location alone. Ottawa offered a sort of compromise, simply because it straddled the borders of Upper and Lower Canada (Ontario and Quebec). Up until then, the obvious antagonism between Upper and Lower Canada had forced the United Provinces of Canada's legislature to give Toronto and Montreal "turns" hosting its meetings.

Generally seen as a proper and sober provincial city with lots of grey-flannelled bureaucrats, Ottawa got a little less stodgy in the 1960s. Some say it was thanks to Canada's increasingly independent spirit and budding nationalism. Others say the new National Arts Centre, the growing number of ethnic restaurants and the renovation of areas like the Byward Market had plenty to do with Ottawa's new demeanour.

Next page: Canada's parliament was born in 1867 and was based on the British parliamentary system. Today, it represents Canadians from all parts of the world in the country's two official languages.

*An aerial view of the **Parliament Buildings**, also known as "**The Hill**".*

Parliament Hill

Most people know that Ottawa is Canada's capital and home to the federal government. They recognize the **Parliament Buildings** because they're often seen on television and on stamps. There is a real sense of history here - the Parliament Buildings possess a certain gothic romance.

"The Hill" revels in the pomp and pageantry of the **Changing of the Guard Ceremony** while hosting fun-filled, free concerts, fireworks and more. It's no wonder "The Hill" remains one of the Capital's most popular tourist attractions.

High above Ottawa, Parliament Hill's **Centre**, **East** and **West Blocks**, stand sentinel over this stately city and the scenic Ottawa River, taking in the sweeping panorama and offering one of Ottawa's best views.

Making their home in splendid chambers in the Centre Block, the Senate and House of Commons shape and mould Canadian law for all Canadians, present and future.

*Pomp and pageantry - the **Royal Canadian Mounted Police** - a loved and respected symbol of Canada.*

The Centre Block's great **Peace Tower** houses a magnificent 53-bell carillon, a massive clock and the **Memorial Chamber** commemorating Canada's heroic war dead. Stones from World War I were hauled to form the third floor in 1927, bringing a bit of the past into the present for future generations.

The Centre Block, replaced the original building destroyed by fire in 1916, but architects, Pearson and Marchand, ordered what one newspaper deemed a "hurried and secret demolition". Originally, they'd planned to keep the old walls and rebuild with some changes but, in fact, they created a new steel-framed building half as big as its predecessor.

Nevertheless, the walls are built from the same sandstone of Nepean Township, 20 kilometres west of Ottawa. Reminiscent of the British Houses of Parliament with the pointed, arched windows, steep roofs and corner turrets, the Gothic Revival style is continued.

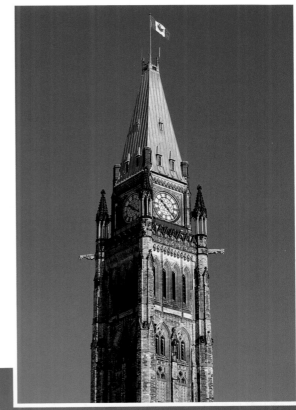

The Peace Tower houses the Memorial Chamber, a shrine to all Canadians who died in service to their country. ➤

The first Houses of Parliament were built in 1865 but destroyed by fire in 1916. The first session of Parliament in the newly constructed buildings took place in February 1920.

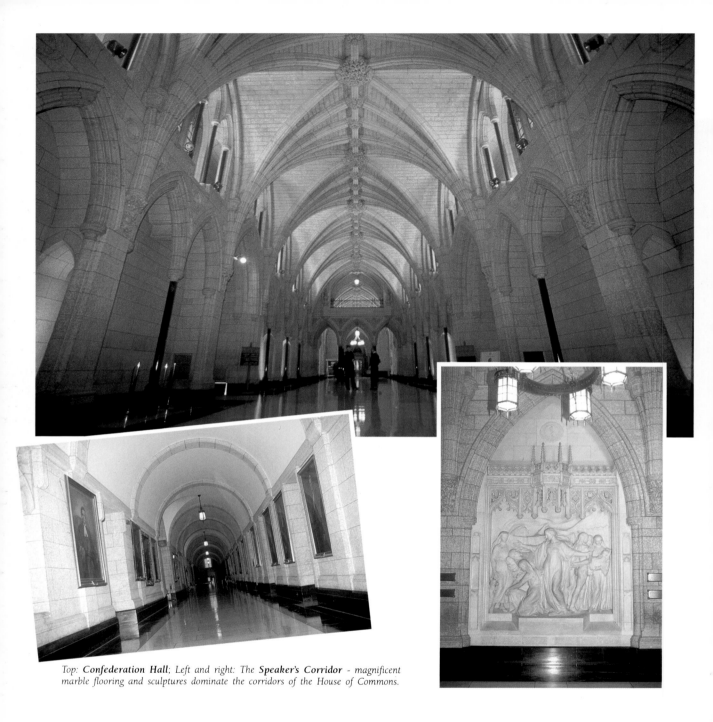

*Top: **Confederation Hall**; Left and right: The **Speaker's Corridor** - magnificent marble flooring and sculptures dominate the corridors of the House of Commons.*

The Centre Block's **Parliamentary Library** is open to the public only as part of guided tours, but its ornate interior, divided into 16 bays, each three stories high, is well worth the visit. The arcade galleries original glass floors were replaced with wood after women joined the Library staff. As you leave the library, note the steel doors painted to resemble wood. They saved the library from the 1916 fire.

Pearson's interpretation of Neo-Gothic designs, a fascinating contrast to architects Stent and Laver's less restrained East and West Blocks, gives the

Centre Block a more solid, imposing presence.

The 90 metre high Peace Tower was modified in 1981 to accommodate the world's first two-directional elevator. Specially designed by the Otis Elevator Company, the cab pivots like the seat of a ferris wheel, rising straight up for several metres and finishes its remaining 20-metre journey horizontally.

Back in 1865, the East and West Blocks that flank the Centre Block were home to virtually every government department, all cabinet ministers, the Prime Minister and the Governor-General.

*The **Library of Parliament** where Queen Victoria still reigns.* ➤

The **House of Commons**. *This is where most of the country's business is debated and determined by the Prime Minister, Leader of the Opposition and their elected members of parliament.*

In 1865, there were just 264 people in the public service. Today, more than 100,000 public servants are scattered among dozens of buildings in Ottawa and Hull, and only some members of Parliament, the Senate and their staffs use the buildings.

The West Block was the site of the first telephone conversation in Ottawa. Prime Minister Alexander Mackenzie's private secretary, William Buckingham, recited the Lord's Prayer to him over the phone in September 1877. Immediately following this telecommunicating success Mackenzie and Governor-General Lord Dufferin authorized a two-mile telephone line from Rideau Hall, the Governor-General's residence, to Mackenzie's office in the West Block.

Varied Nepean sandstone is brightened with red Potsdam sandstone, and the two combined, between the first and second-storey windows, resemble a Victorian crazy-quilt. Designed in the Civil Gothic style by architects Stent and Laver, the windows and doors are trimmed with the more sober buff Ohio sandstone.

Wooden dormer windows were added in the 1870s to make the attics usable and they work with rich decorative carving and grotesque

gargoyles to add visual interest to the roof area. On the East Block's southwest corner tower and in other areas, the openings are often seen as the eyes and nose of a face.

The West Block originally looked much like its twin, but Canada's first chief architect, Thomas Seaton Scott, under the direction of Prime Minister Alexander Mackenzie, added the west front from 1874 to 1878. The imposing Mackenzie Tower was Ottawa's tallest structure, until the Peace Tower was built 50 years later.

All three government buildings sported variegated slate roofs, which were replaced with copper in the 1940s.

*The **Senate Chamber**. All bills passed by the House of Commons must also pass through the Senate before becoming law.*

Museums and Galleries

When most people plan a trip to Ottawa they think of it as getting to "know" Canada. Everyone likes to take a tour through the historic buildings of Parliament Hill and see first hand those famous doors and chambers made so familiar by television. But some of the most exciting tours to take in Ottawa are through the city's many museums and art galleries. So while discovering Canada's political heritage discover something about what it means to be Canadian as well.

The memorable **National Gallery of Canada** boasts the world's most comprehensive collection of Canadian art as well as galleries filled with European, American and Asian masterpieces. It's both a satisfying and enlightening experience.

The Euro-Gallery in the **National Art Gallery of Canada***.*

The impressive architecture of the **National Art Gallery of Canada***.*

*The interior of the former Rideau **St. Convent** now housed in the Gallery.*

The Gallery's unique architectural design resembles that of the Parliamentary Library.

The Water Court - *a quiet corner under the sun.*

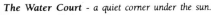

The Gallery's interior was designed to create a feeling of space and light.

*Complementing the gothic architecture of old Ottawa, the stunning design of the **Canadian Museum of Civilization** in Hull adds great contrast to the Ottawa skyline.*

Canada's ancestry is beautifully displayed in the museum's Grand Hall Indian art exhibit.

Architecturally stunning, the **Canadian Museum of Civilization** in Hull traces Canada's intriguing history from prehistoric times to the present. Visitor's come face-to-face with longhouses and totem poles from the northwest coast, life-size reconstructions of historic Canadian scenes and overwhelming, larger-than-life movies in both IMAX and OMNIMAX wide-screen formats.

The museum, located on the banks of the Ottawa River, is also an attractive venue for dance performances, musical groups, theatrical presentations and many celebrations and festivals.

Canadian Museum of Civilization.

The museum's architecture and sculptures celebrate Canada's artists.

Framed against the contemporary design of the museum, former dwellings of Canada's Northwest Coast Indians.

*Experience the history of Canadian flight at the **National Aviation Museum**.*

Canadians get to toot their own horns at **The National Museum of Science and Technology**, applauding their own accomplishments and their incredible effects on this country as well as nations worldwide. Even better, kids of all ages learn about human ingenuity through hands-on activities, demonstrations and working exhibits.

The unforgettable scent of fresh-cut summer hay and the sun dancing on dust motes become a reality for city slickers, and a lovely memory for farm folk at the **Agriculture Museum and Central Experimental Farm**.

Conflict defined Canada, shaping its borders, determining the languages and choosing ethnic heritage. But at **The Canadian War Museum**, the conflict of war is never glorified. Instead, it's presented as an integral part of Canadian heritage.

Canada in Space: Destination Earth exhibit at the
National Museum of Science and Technology.

*Top: Be a part of Canada's peacekeeping efforts, her glories and her conflicts, through the years at the **Canadian War Museum**.
Bottom left & right: See how man took to the skies at the **National Aviation Museum**. Exhibits of over 100 aircraft are on display.*

At **The National Aviation Museum** Canada's best collection of vintage aircraft includes remnants of the famed and legendary Avro Arrow, a feisty World War II Spitfire and a loving reproduction of the strikingly delicate Silver Dart.

An 1859 Colonial Bank of Canada $4.00 bill on display at the **Currency Museum**, Bank of Canada.

Dated 1714, a New France, 50 livres note. Fascinating exhibits of money from the Old and New Worlds at the **Currency Museum**.

Money - it's fascinating, precisely because it really does make the world go round and has since the beginning of time. Come face-to-face with this slice of history at the **Currency Museum** with notes and coins from today's world as well as the Old and New Worlds.

Bearing witness in a reconstructed railway tunnel, this collection at Canada's first museum of photography shows off more than 158,000 images, giving added insight into different worlds through **The Canadian Museum of Contemporary Photography**.

In its past life as a small, early 1800s hospital, **The Royal Canadian Mint** was a source of great solace for the cholera victims as they were carried from river steamers, but since 1905, extraordinary

*Explore the world of nature at the **Canadian Museum of Nature**.*

*Housed in a reconstructed railway tunnel, the **Canadian Museum of Contemporary Photography** exhibits works of Canada's well-known and not-so-known artists.*

special commemorative coins, medals and bullion have been struck here.

The **Canadian Museum of Nature** takes visitors on a timely voyage, facing life and death issues, and explores the fascinating world of nature and the poisonous challenges facing the environment.

24 Sussex Drive is home to the Prime Minister of Canada.

Ottawa's Main Attractions

Now home and haven to Canada's Prime Minister, **24 Sussex Drive**, a gracious 30-room mansion, was once the pride and joy of a whole slew of wealthy lumber barons. Now more than 125 years old, it's been an "official residence" for close to 50 years.

"The Castle", also known as **Rideau Hall**, the impressive residence of Canada's Governor General, the Queen's representative, sits across the street from the Prime Minister's home. Scottish in styling, Rideau Hall has 88 acres worth of exquisite grounds with elegant, formal gardens, lush lawns and a lovely arboretum. Through the sweet summer months, a small scale Changing the Guard ceremony is a charming tradition.

The 1930s were dirty indeed, but the **Supreme Court of Canada** was erected in spite of the Depression and Princess Elizabeth (now the Queen) crossed the ocean to lay the traditional cornerstone in 1939.

Rolling out the red carpet in preparation
for an official welcome at **24 Sussex Drive**.

*The highest court in the land, the **Supreme Court of Canada**.*

***Rideau Hall** is the residence of the Queen of Canada's official Canadian representative, the Governor-General. Inset: The greenhouse at **Rideau Hall**.*

*The **Chateau Laurier** brightens up a snowy night.*

*The **Chateau Laurier**, in the background, with the **Conference Centre** in the foreground, overlooks the **Rideau Canal**.*

A well-loved landmark, with its fairy tale turrets, steep copper roof and imposing granite and sandstone walls, the **Chateau Laurier**, built in 1912 by the Grand Trunk Railway, is one of the city's favourite spots.

Cathedral-Basilica of Notre Dame - with its graceful spires - is as awesome inside as outside with an exquisitely detailed interior to which labourers and craftsmen devoted some 50 years, long after construction began around 1840. True artists in their own right, many of the sculptors who worked on the Parliament Buildings quite literally had a hand in creating more than 200 statues surrounding Notre Dame's main altar.

Steeped in ancient and more recent histories, Laurier House was the home of two Canadian Prime Ministers, Sir Wilfred Laurier (from 1897 to 1919) and William Lyon Mackenzie King (from 1923 to 1950). Prime Minister from 1963 to 1968, Nobel Peace Prize winner, Lester B. Pearson, is honoured in the second floor wing with a re-creation of his study.

In 1905, 300 Scottish master stonemasons and stonecutters arrived to build architect David Ewart's castle-like **Victoria Memorial Museum**, now the **Museum of Nature**. Like the Scottish masons who came to build the Rideau Canal in the 1820s, many of these men settled in and around Ottawa and went on to build public buildings, such as the Connaught Building, the War Museum and the Mint, as well as private homes.

*The stately **Cathedral - Basilica** of **Notre Dame** on Sussex Drive.*

*Solid, stately and serious looking, like its namesake, the **Victoria Memorial Museum** has weathered the years well and is now known as the **Museum of Nature**.*

Above left: Shop or rest awhile in **Sparks Street Mall**.
Above: The **Noonday Gun** on Major's Hill.

A rough and tumble lumber town in its early years, Ottawa later developed a charm and beauty all its own, and the incarnation of **Major's Hill** as a park was part of that process.

In Rockcliffe Park, one of the oldest, largest and most distinguished city green spaces, you'll find a whimsical stone gazebo and pleasing gardens.

In their distinguished red coats, sitting solemnly astride their mounts, the Mounties run through their drills at the Canadian Police College grounds. In 1873, the North-West Mounted Police were created by the young Federal government to enforce the law in the wild west. Before long, everyone knew that the Mounties "always get their man" and in 1918, they became a nationwide force.

Canada's incredible heritage, often full of surprises, is published, preserved and promoted, for everyone who cares about Canada, at the **National Library of Canada** in lovingly preserved books, periodicals, sound recordings and other materials.

Canada's **Native heritage** is evident
in many of the parks in and around Ottawa.

The **National Library of Canada** archives news, literature and media material to preserve and promote Canadian heritage.

The oldest pedestrian mall in the country - if only the sidewalks of the **Sparks Street Mall** could talk, what a tangled tale they'd weave.

Ships routinely climb the steps of the eight **Ottawa Locks**, marking the Rideau Canal's northern entrance and rising nearly 80 feet, or more than 24 metres.

Sparks Street Mall at night. ➤

Hartwell Locks on the Rideau Canal.

Minto Park, surrounded by elegant homes that are as much a part of the ambience as they were in the 1890s when the park was built, still offers urban dwellers an appreciated respite from the city itself. And it has the honour of being Ottawa's first designated heritage park.

Step into the gracious world of Victorian homes, complete with 19th century-style gas lamps, and let Somerset Village take you to a simpler and very special time.

The straight sheen of water, created as the waters tumble into the Ottawa River, so resembled a sheer curtain, early explorers named these "Rideau Falls"

after the French noun for curtain. Jagged and fierce, the rocks rise from the ridge of the falls like spiky bristles along a hog's spine, hence the name Hog's Back Falls.

The world's longest skating rink, the eight kilo-metre stretch known as The Rideau Canal, has made skating in the crisp winter air a tried and true tradition.

Honeymooning newlyweds, Bradish and Lamira Billings, canoed down the Rideau River in 1813, becoming the first settlers to build south of the river. Little did they know, their frame home would be known as the elegant Billings Estate Museum.

Permanent Tributes to Past, Present and Future Canadians

Some of Canada's distinguished citizens, loyal subjects and future architects of the country. Clockwise from page 30: Samuel de Champlain, Lester B. Pearson, Terry Fox, Servicemen of the Peacekeeping Memorial, "Balancing", and Canada's Future.

*Known for excellence in journalism, international affairs and architecture - **Carleton University**.*

*The **University of Ottawa** is Canada's oldest bilingual post-secondary institution of learning.*

Ottawa's Universities

Besides being Canada's political centre, Ottawa is also well-known for its institutions of higher learning - in particular **Carleton** and **Ottawa Univeristies**.

Carleton began as a wartime charity. It was founded in 1942 by local businessmen and senior civil servants who saw higher education as a worthy cause. Today, though small enough to be personal and accessible, Carleton offers undergraduate degrees in more than 50 disciplines and academic specialities.

From its very beginnings, the then College of Bytown was small but showed great promise. Now, as the University of Ottawa, located in the heart of the nation's capital, the University has emerged as a vibrant centre of learning with a total population, including students, teaching and support staff, of 30,000.

Canada Day on "The Hill".

Festivals and Celebrations

The city keeps more than its 920,000 residents hopping with festivals and celebrations year-round. Visitors and locals dance, sing - and keep the energy high from season to season. For a cultural experience, they all wander through world-class museums and traipse through an array of renown art galleries.

Every snowflake is unique, every icicle has its own special elegance and every February, **Winterlude** celebrates winter's glories revelling in northern lifestyles. All take great pleasure in magical sleigh rides, spectacular snow and ice sculpture competitions and sporting events that include such novelties as barrel jumping and the Great Canadian Bed Race.

*Visitors of the Tulip Festival show and admire the decorated boats in the **Flotilla Parade** on the Rideau Canal.* ➤

Top: Snow-rowing takes on olympic proportions during **Winterlude**.

Left: Up, up and away from the snow for a while.

Middle right: **Winterlude** becomes more than just skates and skis as the Ice-capades thrill an audience on a wintery evening.

Bottom right: Professional and amateur ice-sculptors share their talent.

The Canadian Tulip Festival brings spring and colour to brighten Ottawa after a long winter.

Aaahhh - the world's tulip capital - no, not Amsterdam, but Canada's own Ottawa bursts into spring with the resplendent bloom of brightly painted tulips. It's a lush array of spring's best-loved floral celebrations for the **Canadian Tulip Festival**. To thank Canadians for offering Holland's Princess Juliana refuge from the Nazis during the royal birth of Princess Margriet back in 1943, the Dutch sent tulips rather than their famed windmills or cheeses. Canada did more than give their majesties a hospital room. The Canadian government declared that modest room a territory of the Netherlands and the Dutch flag was flown from the Parliament Buildings, the only foreign flag ever allowed on the Peace Tower. Every spring, Holland's gift to Canada gives again, reminding Canadians of the Ottawa-born princess across the Atlantic.

Early, average and late flowering varieties are mixed to keep Ottawa spectacular through the spring season, says Ottawa's official tulip spokesperson. Those blooms always blossom bright and strong, because every two years, the tulips are dug up, composted and replaced to keep them disease-free. More than 1 million tulips flower to warm Ottawa's spring-starved soul after every long, hard winter.

The energy of dance, the passion of theatre, the artist's vision and the joy of music, are all at the **Canada Post Promenade for the Arts**, giving everyone incredibly vibrant, performance-packed days and exciting soirees.

*Ballooning aficionados at the **Gatineau Hot Air Balloon Festival**.*

Floating with grace and touched with many colours, hot air balloons drift gently skyward, filling the heavens with their own special magic at the **Gatineau Hot Air Balloon Festival** every Labour Day Weekend.

Wildly popular, original, dynamic and exceptionally distinctive, the **Festival Franco-Ontarien** spotlights French artists who are truly the creme-de-la-creme in more than 300 wonderful shows.

Skillful and daring, experts in their flying machines pilot their crafts through aerobatic stunts that defy gravity, death and quite possibly, sanity at **The National Capital Air Show**.

As steamy as hot summer nights, the Ottawa International Jazz Festival takes the music to the people under twinkling stars and black velvet nights in the streets and parks and in intimate night clubs all over the city. Renown international and local musical artists "Jazz It Up" with everything from avant garde fusion to world beat and traditional rhythm and blues.

*Dare-devils perform at the **National Capital Air Show**.*

*The shuttlecraft "lands" at the **National Capital Air Show**.*

The Rideau Canal is a most popular venue year-round for festival celebrations.

The open-air **Astrolabe Theatre's** mission was to bring people to Ottawa's core for the dazzling sound and light shows given during Canada's Centennial of Confederation in 1967. Some 30 years later, it's still luring them with fabulous free concerts by chart-topping Canadian artists.

Families have fun together skating up and down the Rideau Canal.

The Canadian Tulip Festival is celebrated in the month of May each year.

The **Royal Canadian Mounted Police** are popular participants at all Ottawa festivals and celebrations.

The **Homelands Multi-cultural Festival** brings Canada's many cultures and traditions together each May.

Experience the world's many tantalizing tastes, sweet sounds and fascinating traditions, as well as spirited music and dance from diverse cultures as a host of countries welcome all to the excitement of their various pavilions at the **Homelands Multi-Cultural Festival** every May.

Across Canada, people eagerly anticipate the late summer exhibitions, but it's bittersweet because from coast-to-coast, they herald that tried and true back-to-school and holidays-are-over kind of real-life seriousness. Be sure you relish the rolling, rollicking midway, the globally inspired International Promenade and last blast concerts at **The Central Canada Exhibition**, before that first lick of old man winter's frost.

Back in 1867, Canada's government spent just $500 to whoop it up on July 1st, Canada Day, and although public reaction back then was mixed, today Canadians from sea to shining sea celebrate Canada Day with great joy and affection.

Sparkling and shining in an adult's eye as much as every child's, Confederation Boulevard glimmers and gleams with thousands of twinkling lights during "**Christmas Lights across Canada**" in December and January.

*The facade of an old **English Abbey** was brought to Canada by Mackenzie King. The ruins still sit in the grounds of his estate in **Gatineau Park**.*

*This old facade of a house was once the local tinsmiths' house and now graces the front of the **Tin House Court**.*

Ottawa's Architecture

The picturesque **Gothic Revival** design of the Parliament Buildings and the architects' use of local materials in them inspired contemporary architects and builders to use these materials with confidence and pride. Quarries, sandpits, brick works, foundries, lumber mills and skilled craftsmen busily provided homes for the growing population.

A white marble deposit in Rockcliffe meant that by 1872, Thomas Clark's brick works were producing the red and white brick used so extensively in the capital region.

Another entrepreneur, Thomas Woodburn, a carpenter at MacKay's New Edinburgh mills, effectively advertised his trade and skill in his Victorian Gothic double at 73-73 MacKay Street in 1874. His ornate carpentry work included fanciful wishbone-shaped trim and pretty wooden porches.

By the late 1800s, the accepted Gothic Revival style, with its ornate, steeply gabled roofs, pointed arch windows, gingerbread trim, bay and oriel windows, was being re-interpreted. A fanciful extension of gothic, the Queen Anne style was popular for houses with pretty external silhouettes, which translated into a more flexible interior floor plan.

Old architectural treasures like these heritage homes are carefully preserved in Ottawa.

Downtown Ottawa is a mecca for conventions and conferences because there is so much to see and a great selection of hotels.

Centretown, a vital part of downtown Ottawa, is home to many young urban professionals, who relish the easy access to lively Elgin Street with its art galleries, cafes, gourmet food shops, book shops and restaurants. Turn-of-the-century mansions, in their new purposes as guest homes and bed-and-breakfasts, welcome tourists, giving them a taste of the city's true flavour.

New Edinburgh, near Sandy Hill, was once the Village of New Edinburgh, owned by Thomas MacKay, the stonemason who worked with Colonel By on the Rideau Canal. MacKay Street is his namesake and Charles, John, Victoria and Alexander Streets are named for his children. The MacKay Mill and industrial complex were based here, as were many of MacKay's labourers. Many of their descendants still live in New Edinburgh, giving this quaint village within the capital a strong Scottish feel. An intricate network of lanes, lovingly renovated frame and brick homes and the beautiful Minto Bridge give New Edinburgh a unique character.

In Ottawa, people from around the world work and play in both English and French. Of course, you'll also hear rapid-fire conversations in Chinese, German and Spanish, just a few of the "unofficial" Canadian languages you'll hear tripping from locals' tongues. The cultural mosaic is alive and well in Ottawa, which was blessed with a striking natural beauty.

Everyone keeps the local economy humming, shopping 'till they drop in the **Byward Market** and other well-dressed retail areas. It's easy to revel in the one-of-a-kind pieces handcrafted by local artisans, as well as fine goods from around the world.

Of course, with Ottawa's multi-cultural population, virtually every cuisine known to humankind is within easy gastronomic reach. Take your taste buds on a world tour right here in Ottawa.

Ottawa - the best of many worlds, from the cultural to the historical, from the best of city life to the great outdoors.

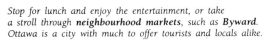

Stop for lunch and enjoy the entertainment, or take
a stroll through **neighbourhood markets**, such as Byward.
Ottawa is a city with much to offer tourists and locals alike.

Ottawa's leaders of the ice - the **Ottawa Senators.**

Sports

The Ottawa Senators were one of the original teams to form the first "National Hockey League" - and they were a big success! So big a success that the coveted trophy, The Stanley Cup, was donated by Lord Stanley of Preston while residing in Ottawa, where he cheered on his favourite team. Fans loved the Senators and Ottawa became a hockey town. That's why it was so devastating when the franchise, struggling during the height of the depression, left Ottawa for St. Louis to become the Eagles.

Ottawa was, of course, thrilled to have their Ottawa Senators back on the ice in 1992 after the NHL granted an expansion franchise to Terrace Investments Limited, an Ottawa firm dedicated to bringing back the Senators. The team, after a 58 year absence, won their first game back, beating the Montreal Canadiens 5-3. Now, loved once again, the Senators are known as a team with character, team spirit and physical and mental toughness.

The Senators play home games at the Corel Centre. ➤

*Ottawa and its regions offer some of the best **whitewater rafting** vanues.*

***Cycling** events can test competitors' strengths
and skills when they are caught in a summer shower.*

***Cross-country skiing** is stimulating in Ottawa's hardy winters.*

Casino de Hull offers patrons the elegant atmosphere and facilities of a world-class gambling establishment.

Casino de Hull

Casino de Hull offers everything to ensure the glamour and excitement anticipated by enthusiastic thrill-seekers. Housed in a futuristic structure, only minutes from **Parliament Hill**, it is a favourite destination for tourists and locals alike.

A dress-code is in effect, resulting in a true casino-style atmosphere. And while the gambling options are world-class, there are many other reasons to experience Casino de Hull. Visitors can enjoy thousands of tropical plants, indoor pools, waterfalls and spectacular decor. The gourmet restaurant, **Le Baccara**, will satisfy every taste with its fine cuisine. Or there are a wide variety of dishes and a buffet at **Banco**. The casino also boasts a variety of bars including **La marina** which offers a breath-taking view of the majestic 60-meter fountain outside. The **Salon Royal** is the perfect reception hall and **Le 777**, found in the heart of the casino, has an abundance of atmosphere with an oasis of greenery.

Just minutes from downtown Hull and the Parliament Buildings in Ottawa, Casino de Hull is attraction that can't be missed.

Ottawa - a city for all Canadians

Ottawa is a party city. But not just for the parties on "The Hill". Ottawa's residents love the fact that they are surrounded by history. Being the capital city of Canada means that official ceremonies to welcome foreign dignitaries are almost an everyday event. Plus Ottawa is host to some of Canada's most colourful festivals where young and old come together to party and celebrate a great Canadian city.

CONTENTS

Text by
Kara Kuryllowicz

Photography

CANADIAN MUSEUM OF CONTEMPORY PHOTOGRAPHY W.P. McElligott	21b	RONATIONAL ART GALLERY	14, 15
CARLETON UNIVERSITY	35a	NCC/CCN	2, 6b, 10, 12, 17b/c, 19b, 21a/c, 24b, 26b, 28, 29a, 30a, 31a/c, 25c, 36, 38, 2b, 43, 44, 45, 4 48, 49, 53, 58, 60, 61
COMSTOCK/MALAK	24a, 37, 39		
CURRENCY MUSEUM James Zagon	20	OTTAWA TOURISM AND CONVENTION INC.	19c, 42a
L. Fisher	6a, 8, 9b, 16, 17a, 18a, 19a, 25a, 26a, 27, 29b/c, 30b, 31b, 34	Robert Evans	57a/b, 59
		G. Romany	9a
Malak 32/33, 46/47, 62/63	3, 4/5, 7, 11, 13, 22/23,	SCIENCE AND TECHNOLOGY MUSEUM	18b
		SPORTFOCUS/OSHC Teckles/McElligott	56
MASTERFILE G. Black	40/41		
H. Blohm	50/51	UNIVERSITY OF OTTAWA	35b
B. Brooks	Front cover, Back cover		
J. De Nisser	25b	IRVING WEISDORF & CO.	52, 54/55

(Also available in French, German, Spanish, Italian and Japanese)

Copyright © 1995 **Irving Weisdorf & Co. Ltd.** Revised 1999

Printed in Canada